Russia's Economy

Signs of Progress and Retreat on the Transitional Road

Charles Wolf, Jr., Thomas Lang

Prepared for the Office of the Secretary of Defense

 NATIONAL DEFENSE RESEARCH INSTITUTE

The research described in this report was prepared for the Office of the Secretary of Defense (OSD). The research was conducted in the RAND National Defense Research Institute, a federally funded research and development center sponsored by the OSD, the Joint Staff, the Unified Combatant Commands, the Department of the Navy, the Marine Corps, the defense agencies, and the defense Intelligence Community under Contract W74V8H-06-C-0002.

Library of Congress Cataloging-in-Publication Data

Wolf, Charles, 1924–
    Russia's economy : signs of progress and retreat on the transitional road /
Charles Wolf, Thomas Lang.
      p. cm.
    Includes bibliographical references.
    ISBN-13: 978-0-8330-3976-7 (pbk. : alk. paper)
      1. Russia (Federation)—Economic conditions—1991– 2. Russia (Federation)—
Economic policy—1991– I. Lang, Thomas, 1975– II. Title.

HC340.12.W66 2006
330.947—dc22

                                                                                            2006030353

The RAND Corporation is a nonprofit research organization providing objective analysis and effective solutions that address the challenges facing the public and private sectors around the world. RAND's publications do not necessarily reflect the opinions of its research clients and sponsors.

RAND® is a registered trademark.

© Copyright 2006 RAND Corporation

Published 2006 by the RAND Corporation
1776 Main Street, P.O. Box 2138, Santa Monica, CA 90407-2138
1200 South Hayes Street, Arlington, VA 22202-5050
4570 Fifth Avenue, Suite 600, Pittsburgh, PA 15213-2665
RAND URL: http://www.rand.org/
To order RAND documents or to obtain additional information, contact
Distribution Services: Telephone: (310) 451-7002;
Fax: (310) 451-6915; Email: order@rand.org

Preface

The research described in this monograph was sponsored by the Office of the Secretary of Defense and conducted within the International Security and Defense Policy Center of the RAND Corporation's National Defense Research Institute, a federally funded research and development center sponsored by the Office of the Secretary of Defense, the Joint Staff, the Unified Combatant Commands, the Department of the Navy, the Marine Corps, the defense agencies, and the defense Intelligence Community.

This research should be of concern to those in the Defense Department and in the larger national security community whose interests include trends in Russia's economic growth, the effects of global energy markets on these trends, the mixed evidence of economic reform, and the impact of these developments on Russia's defense spending.

For more information on RAND's International Security and Defense Policy Center, contact the Director, James Dobbins. He can be reached by e-mail at James_Dobbins@rand.org; by phone at 703-413-1100, extension 5134; or by mail at the RAND Corporation, 1200 South Hayes Street, Arlington, VA 22202. More information about RAND is available at www.rand.org.

Contents

Figures

Tables

Summary

Of the numerous economies considered to be "transitional," Russia—
with a gross domestic product (GDP) about one-fifth that of China,
but a per capita product twice that of China—has the second largest.
Exactly where the Russian economy lies in the market-oriented gamut
of transitioning economies, however, is not yet clear: between, say,
Cuba, Belarus, Uzbekistan, and Vietnam at one end, and some of the
Balkan and central European states and China at the other end? Also
unclear, and probably more important, is the pace of the Russian economy's transition and whether it is headed forward, toward market-oriented, decentralized resource allocation; backward, toward centralized,
state-controlled allocation; or is, instead, oscillating between these two.
These issues are controversial and vigorously debated within Russia.

Despite some statistical shadows and ambiguities, it is evident
that Russia's aggregate economic growth since 1998 has been relatively
strong. In 2004, President Putin announced a goal of doubling the
Russian GDP over the next 10 years, implying an annual growth rate
of more than 7 percent, which is only slightly above the average rate
realized by the Russian economy since 1998. Since that date, Russia's
annual GDP growth rate of over 6 percent has been about three times
that of the (unweighted) average of the other G8 members: Japan,
Germany, France, Canada, Italy, the United Kingdom, and the United
States.

Within this context, our study focused on four questions whose
answers shed light on some of the ambiguities surrounding Russia's
status as a transitional economy:

1. How much of Russia's relatively strong, yet varying, economic growth is attributable to oil and natural gas prices, production, and exports?
2. To what extent have other institutional and structural changes—such as the growth of private enterprise and marketization—affected Russia's economic growth and its prospects?
3. What have been the scope and composition of Russia's economic transactions with several of its trading partners, specifically the Central Asian states (Kazakhstan, Uzbekistan, Turkmenistan, Tajikistan, and Kyrgyzstan), the "proliferation-risk" countries (Iran and North Korea), and China?
4. How has the economy's transition affected Russia's defense spending, defense industry, and arms exports?

To address the first question, we reviewed extensive data on oil and natural gas prices, production, and export revenues, and the links among them. We conclude that between one-third and two-fifths of the variance in Russian economic growth in the past decade is explained by changes in oil and natural gas prices and their concomitant effects on aggregate production and export revenues.

In addressing the second question, on other institutional and structural changes associated with the Russian economy's transitional progress, we focused on the impressive increase since 1996 in the number of privately owned enterprises and the volume of employment in the private sector, comparing these numbers with those for the state-owned and the mixed public-private sectors.

We also looked at the enhancement of Russia's sovereign debt status from "junk" status to investment grade by the major securities' rating agencies as a complementary indicator of transitional progress.

For the third question, we reviewed the debate on Russia's expanded economic relations with the Central Asian states and with China. It is our opinion that expanded economic relations in these cases are more appropriately and objectively viewed as a reflection of the Russian economy's relatively high rate of economic growth, rather than as a significant instrument of economic penetration and expanded Russian economic influence in these countries. Russia's exercise of economic "leverage" through its energy exports is a legitimate U.S. concern, but one that is likely to be limited—at least in the medium and longer term—by the fact that these transactions are increasingly occurring at market rather than subsidized prices. As for the two proliferation-risk countries, Iran and North Korea, Russia's expanded economic relations with them inevitably add resources to their ongoing and prospective weapons of mass destruction programs, a spillover effect that should be of serious concern to the United States.

Finally, with respect to the fourth question, we conclude that Russia's defense sectors—military spending, the defense industry, and arms exports—have thus far not prospered in the course of Russia's recent and continuing economic transition. These sectors experienced acute resource deprivation in the immediate post-Soviet period. Based on a brief review of the relevant data, it appears that the trough of this deprivation has passed and that these sectors are likely to experience larger and continuing benefits from the sustained growth of the Russian economy.

Acknowledgments

We have benefited from comments made on an earlier draft of this monograph by RAND colleagues Jeremy Azrael and Keith Crane, and by Anders Aslund of the Institute for International Economics. Of course, none of these worthy scholars bears any responsibility for the findings and judgments expressed herein.

We also express our appreciation to Jeri O'Donnell for editorial assistance that makes the story more intelligible, and to Suzanne Benedict for integrating successive, complicated revisions of the text, tables, and figures.

Abbreviations

ADB	Asian Development Bank
CBR	Central Bank of the Russian Federation
CIA	Central Intelligence Agency
EBRD	European Bank for Reconstruction and Development
EIA	Energy Information Administration
EIU	Economist Intelligence Unit
EU	European Union
GDP	gross domestic product
IISS	International Institute for Strategic Studies
IMF	International Monetary Fund
KGB	Intelligence and internal security agency of former Soviet Union
NGO	non-governmental organization
PPP	purchasing power parity
Q	quarter
R^2	R squared
S&P	Standard and Poor's

SIPRI   Stockholm International Peace Research Institute

CHAPTER ONE

Introduction

Russia's economy—or, more accurately, its political economy—has in recent years been replete with both bad news and good news. The bad news stems from evidence of the central government's reversion toward authoritarian intervention in the economy: the breakup of the privately held oil giant, Yukos, and government seizure of its assets, thereby abrogating property rights; the bending of the legal system to prosecute and incarcerate for massive tax fraud Yukos's former principal owner and Putin adversary, Mikhail Khodorkovsky, and his deputy, Paton Lebedev; the takeover by state-owned companies of private companies outside as well as inside the energy sector;[1] the Kremlin's ambivalent signals about permitting or prohibiting foreign or domestic owner-ship of key Russian corporate assets; the acquisition of major media outlets by state-controlled companies; and the government's decision to appoint both the formerly elected governors of the federation's 88 regions and the heads of key "non-government" organizations.

The good news is no less abundant: the growth of private enter-prise and its encouragement (sometimes actively, sometimes passively) by government; the husbanding rather than dissipating of economic rents from high oil and natural gas prices, thereby raising Russia's sov-ereign debt status to investment grade; the enactment and sustainment of a simplified, lower, and flatter income tax system; and an accompa-nying matrix of policy pronouncements favorable to foreign investment in Russia, notwithstanding the contrary signals mentioned above. The

---

[1]   For examples of other takeovers and interventions, see Chapter Four, fn. 2.

combined effect of the good news is to accelerate Russia's transitional economic progress.

Transitional Economies

An economy is said to be "transitional" when what was previously a centrally planned system in which the central government and its bureaucracies made major resource allocation decisions begins moving toward a decentralized system in which such decisions are increasingly made by individuals, competing firms, and market-driven forces.[2]

Fifteen years after the demise of the Soviet Union, Russia's economy can still be appropriately characterized as transitional. Of the numerous economies generally considered to be transitional, Russia's is the second largest—Russia's gross domestic product (GDP) is about one-fifth that of China, while its per capita product is about twice that of China.[3] However, precisely where Russia lies in the broad spectrum of transitional economies—between, say, Cuba, Belarus, Uzbekistan, and Vietnam at one end, and some of the Balkan and central Euro-

---

[2]   The economic development literature abounds in articles on and references to transitional economies, and American universities abound in centers and institutes that focus on transitional economies—for example, Padma Desai's Center for Transition Economies, Columbia University; The William Davidson Institute, University of Michigan; Institutional Reform and Informal Sector Center, University of Maryland; Stanford Center for International Development, Stanford University.

[3]   These ratios reflect purchasing power parity (PPP) exchange rates. Using market exchange rates boosts both ratios. See Table A-1, in the Appendix, for these comparisons. At the end of 2005, China's National Bureau of Statistics announced that China's GDP figures for 2004 had been underestimated by 16.4 percent, principally because of an insufficient allowance for output of health, housing, and other services. Allowing for this change obviously would increase the ratio between China's and Russia's GDPs in dollars while reducing the ratio between Russia's and China's per capita GDPs.

pean states and China at the opposite end—is not entirely clear.[4] Egor Gaidar, a distinguished economist and former Russian prime minister, has conjectured that Russia's full transition to a market-based economy is likely to take as long as three generations, about 75 years, because the country has had such a long "duration of the Socialist period and the distortions connected with it" (Gaidar, 2003). Nonetheless, Russia has been recognized by the United States and the European Union (EU) as a "market economy," a status that ostensibly makes a country less likely to have "market economies" impose "anti-dumping" or other protectionist measures on its exports."[5]

A vehement debate currently under way among Russians partly reflects the emphasis being placed on either the good news or the bad news. The sharply different emphases of the two sides suggest both their subjective preferences and the objective benchmarks they have adopted. The debate also highlights disagreement about the reliability of certain official data—notably, whether the striking evidence of private-sector growth portrayed by official statistics is credible.[6] On this point, the "bad news" side of the debate contends that the level of state ownership, production, and employment prevailing in the Rus-

---

[4] Until the early years of the 21st century, more than two dozen economies were classified as transitional. Eight of these (the Czech Republic, Estonia, Hungary, Latvia, Lithuania, Poland, Slovakia, and Slovenia) are now members of the EU and hence are considered by the EU to be market economies. Three others (Bulgaria, Croatia, and Romania) are being considered for EU membership. Hence, according to the European Bank for Reconstruction and Development's (EBRD's) "composite transition index," the cohort of transitional economies has shrunk in recent years. Russia currently has a rating of 3-minus on the EBRD's 4-point scale, which reflects the standards of the EU's industrialized market economies.

[5] It is notable that Russia is not a member of the World Trade Organization, and it is not implausible to infer that political considerations, no less than economic ones, have affected Russia's accreditation as a market economy.

[6] See Chapter Four.

sian economy is at least as large in 2006 as it was before the Khodor-kovsky arrest in 2002.[7]

In articulating what has been referred to above as the bad-news position, Evgeny Yasin, one of its staunchest proponents, as well as a distinguished Russian economist and former Minister of Economy, observed in a public lecture in 2005 that

> In mid-2003 . . . measures aimed at strengthening the state's eco-nomic role were implemented, and institutional reforms almost stopped short. These measures were well-known: ruining of Yukos, sentencing M. Khodorkovsky and P. Lebedev; ensuing tax checks and tax claims presented to many companies for past nonpayments; state attempts to strengthen control over the oil and gas and other sectors that are now recognized as strategi-cally important (telecommunications, power engineering). . . . Decrease in business activity is the direct result of the pressure put on businesses since mid-2003. It has also been manifested in shrinking money demand, falling production growth, growing inflation, and resumed export of capital by Russian companies. . . . Trust is easy to destroy but difficult to build. It will take a long time to reclaim the trust of business in authorities and public institutions needed to persuade businesses to take risks and invest their funds and energy in national development. (Yasin, 2005)

In sharp contrast to these views are those of the good-news advo-cates, who aver that the official data on private-sector growth actually *understate* the pace and magnitude of Russia's transition toward private ownership and market-oriented resource allocation. These advocates contend that the understatement results from efforts by private busi-

---

[7] Yasin, 2005. Yasin expressed similarly firm views in conversations with the principal author in Moscow in October 2005. Yasin places the share of state ownership of Russia's assets, GDP, and employment at no less than 40 percent; others (including one of this report's reviewers) contend that this figure is too high. See also the discussion in Chapter Four and, especially, the data in Table 4.1, which show substantially lower and declining figures for state-owned enterprises and employment, and higher figures for the private sector. Also see Yasin and Yakovlev, 2004.

nesses to avoid or reduce their tax liabilities by not registering or by underreporting the scale of their business activities.[8]

This Report

This report sheds light on a few of the ambiguities surrounding Russia's status as a transitional economy. It does so by focusing on the answers to four questions:

1. How much of Russia's relatively strong, though varying, economic growth is attributable to prices, production, and exports of oil and natural gas?
2. To what extent is Russia's strong growth attributable to other institutional and structural changes and, more specifically, to the growth of private enterprise and marketization?
3. What have been the scale and composition of Russia's economic transactions with several of its trading partners: the Central Asian states (Kazakhstan, Uzbekistan, Turkmenistan, Tajikistan, and Kyrgyzstan); the "proliferation-risk" countries (Iran and North Korea); and China?
4. How have Russia's defense spending, defense industry, and arms exports been affected by the economy's transition?

These questions, especially 3 and 4, reflect issues of interest to cognizant decisionmakers in the U.S. Department of Defense.

Chapter Two provides a brief overview of salient indicators of the Russian economy's growth and status from 1995 to 2005. Chapters Three through Six address, respectively, the four questions whose answers shed light on the Russian economy's status. The final chapter, Seven, presents conclusions and implications.

---

[8]   One of those expressing views along these lines is Professor Gennady Chufrin of the Institute of World Economy (conversations with the principal author toward the end of 2005).

The Macroeconomy

After the Soviet Union collapsed in 1990, real output in the Russian economy fell sharply. However, the depth of the fall was overestimated, the reason being that the pre-collapse GDP of the Soviet economy had been overestimated (Aslund, 1990; Rowen and Wolf, 1990). Consequently, observation of the economy's post-collapse level was erroneously inferred to represent a larger drop than actually occurred.

Numerous characteristics of the Soviet economic system contributed to erroneous estimates of its size, including the absence of market-determined prices for final output, the widespread prevalence of hidden inflation, and the frequency of "value-subtracting" rather than "value-added" use of material inputs. As a result, both the quality and the quantity of Soviet output were eroded, and serious doubts arose about the reliability of Soviet statistics (Rosefielde, 2004, pp. 21, 27, 56; Swain, 1990).

To be sure, many sources of unreliability in the Soviet statistics have been corrected in official Russian data since 1991. For example, the incentives impinging on managers of state industry and agriculture to reach or exceed Gosplan's assigned goals during the Soviet period have changed for the better, leading to more-accurate reporting of production data. However, other sources of unreliability, sources that were largely absent in the Soviet era, have been injected into Russian statistics. For example, output and income are underreported to avoid tax liabilities, and various subterfuges are frequently used to circumvent taxable financial transactions. This has resulted in pervasive uncertainties—for instance, about the scale of capital flight that Russia has experienced in recent years, as well as the extent to which this outflow may have exceeded capital inflows to the Russian economy.

Despite the statistical shadows and ambiguities, it seems clear that Russian GDP growth since 1998 has been relatively strong. In 2004, President Putin announced a goal of doubling Russian GDP in the next 10 years.[1] This implies an annual growth rate of more than 7 percent, which is only slightly above the average annual rate realized by the Russian economy (6.6 percent) in the past seven years through 2005, as shown in Tables 2.1 and 2.2.

In 1998, the inflated Russian economy defaulted on $40 billion of its domestic and sovereign debt and depreciated the ruble by 70 percent, from 6 rubles per dollar in 1998 to 21 rubles per dollar after depreciation. Since the hyperinflation and "meltdown" of 1998, recovery and growth of the macroeconomy have been relatively strong, while the exchange rate has floated freely, buoyed by the favorable trend in earnings from oil and gas exports and Russia's surpluses on its current account.

As Figures 2.1 and 2.2 show, Russia's GDP growth since 1999 has substantially exceeded that of the other G8 members (Japan, Germany, France, Canada, Italy, the United Kingdom, and the United States). In 2005, Russia's annual GDP growth was nearly 6 percent, which is three times that of the unweighted average of the other G8 members.

In sum, the Russian economy's aggregate performance during President Putin's tenure between 2000 and 2005 has been relatively favorable. Foreign debt was reduced from 50 percent of Russia's GDP to 30 percent, Russia's debt of $3.3 billion to the International Monetary Fund (IMF) was repaid ahead of schedule in 2005, and $15 billion of the $40 billion owed to its creditors in the Paris Club was also repaid ahead of schedule. Foreign exchange reserves more than tripled and now amount to over $225 billion.

Whether this impressive record should be attributed to increased oil and natural gas prices, production, and exports; to economic reform

---

[1] See Guy Chazan, "Oil Windfall: Russia Is Flush—for Now; Oil Revenue Bolsters Finances but Restructuring Is Neglected," *Wall Street Journal*, November 17, 2004.

Table 2.1
Russia's Gross Domestic Product, 1995–2005

GDP in billions of:	1995	1996	1997	1998	1999	2000	2001	2002	2003	2004	2005
Constant 2002 rubles	8,004.3	7,732.1	7,801.7	7,419.5	7,820.1	8,602.1	9,040.8	9,465.7	10,156.7	10,877.9	11,552.3
Current $ (nom. exch. rates)	337.0	418.7	428.5	282.4	193.6	259.6	310.0	345.5	431.5	581.4	696.0
Constant 2002 $ (PPP rates)	980.2	946.9	955.4	908.6	957.7	1,053.5	1,107.2	1,159.2	1,243.8	1,332.2	1,416.1

SOURCES: World Bank, World Development Indicators 2005, January 2006; GDP deflators, nominal exchange, and PPP rates were obtained from IMF World Economic Outlook database, http://www.imf.org/external/pubs/ft/weo/2005/02/data/index.htm, September 2005.

NOTES: GDP deflators used for 1995 through 2005 are as reported by IMF; nominal exchange rates used for each year represent average ruble/dollar ratio for that year; PPP between rubles and dollars for 1995 through 2005 is as reported by IMF.

Table 2.2
Real GDP Growth Rates in G8 Countries

G8 Country	Real GDP Growth Rate (%)										
	1995	1996	1997	1998	1999	2000	2001	2002	2003	2004	2005
Canada	2.80	1.60	4.20	4.10	5.50	5.20	1.80	3.10	**2.00**	2.90	2.90
France	2.00	1.10	2.30	3.40	3.20	4.10	2.10	1.30	9.90	2.00	1.50
Germany	1.80	1.00	1.70	2.00	1.90	3.10	1.20	0.10	−0.20	1.60	0.80
Italy	2.90	1.10	2.00	1.80	1.70	3.00	1.80	0.40	0.30	1.20	0.00
Japan	2.00	3.40	1.80	−1.00	−0.10	2.40	0.20	−0.30	1.40	2.70	2.00
Russia	−4.10	−3.60	1.40	−5.30	6.30	10.00	5.10	4.70	7.30	7.20	5.50
UK	2.90	2.70	3.20	3.20	3.00	4.00	2.20	2.00	2.50	3.20	1.90
U.S.	2.50	3.70	4.50	4.20	4.40	3.70	0.80	1.60	2.70	4.20	3.50
Avg., G7	2.41	2.09	2.81	2.53	2.80	3.64	1.44	1.17	1.37	2.54	1.80

SOURCE: IMF, http://www.imf.org/external/country/index.htm, December 1, 2005.

NOTE: Growth rates for Russia were taken from IMF so that comparisons among the countries could be based on the same source. Russia's growth rates were compared with those reported by Goskomstat, and the largest difference between sources is 0.05 percent. Unofficial media reports placed Russia's growth in 2005 at 6.4 percent rather than the 5.5 percent shown here and in Figure 2.1. At the start of 2006, when the empirical work for this study was completed, both the IMF and World Bank continued to record the 5.5 percent growth figure, and Goskomstat had not officially announced any change.

during Putin's administration; or to other factors—that is the overall question addressed in Chapters Three and Four.

It is also worth noting that although the indicators of favorable economic performance are impressive, other indicators portend economic vulnerability. Inflation in 2005 proceeded at an annual rate of 11 percent, for example; and capital flight—an indicator of weakened confidence in the Russian economy among holders of ruble assets— was estimated at over $9.4 billion in 2004 and reached an estimated $5.5 billion by the middle of 2005.[2]

---

[2] "Capital Flight Will Amount to $10 Billion in 2005," *The Russian Business Monitor*, September 21, 2005.

Figure 2.1
Russia's Annual GDP Growth Compared with That of Other
G8 Countries, 1998–2005

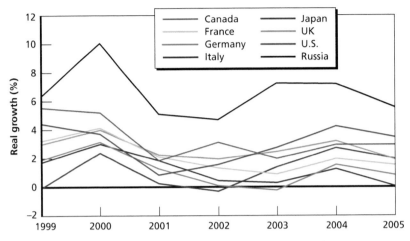

SOURCE: IMF, http://www.imf.org/external/country/index.htm, December 1, 2005.
RAND *MG515-2.1*

Figure 2.2
Russia's Annual GDP Growth Compared with (Unweighted) Average
GDP Growth of Other G8 Countries, 1998–2005

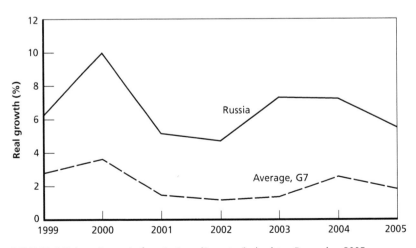

SOURCE: IMF, http://www.imf.org/external/country/index.htm, December 2005.
RAND *MG515-2.2*

This chapter has reviewed only some aspects of the Russian economy's performance, omitting many others, such as employment, labor productivity, trade, and fiscal and monetary indicators. These omissions reflect our focus on the four questions mentioned earlier, as well as other constraints that limited the scope of the study.

CHAPTER THREE

Oil and Natural Gas—Prices, Production, and Exports

As already noted, the Russian economy's performance in the first six years of the 21st century has been significantly stronger than it was in the years immediately after the Soviet Union's collapse. GDP growth was volatile from 2000 to 2005, with the low end of the growth range at 4.7 percent, in 2002, and the upper end at 10.0 percent, in 2000. Despite these fluctuations, average annual growth during this period was 6.6 percent, which is three times the unweighted average growth of the other G8 members.[1] The question of interest is, What accounts for Russia's creditable record?

Numerous explanations can be offered. Some focus on the depressed economic performance in the decade after the Soviet Union collapsed, from which the more recent improvement is simply an unsurprising and natural rebound. In turn, explanations for the previously depressed performance have emphasized the prevalence of hyperinflation during the first years of Russia's transition, as well as the negative effect of the post-collapse "shock therapy" and the predatory activities of the "oligarchs" in the 1990s. Ostensibly these circumstances created abnormal "slack" from which the economy's recent growth has benefited. Other explanations for the economy's improved performance emphasize the growth-promoting effects of fortuitous changes in external circumstances and/or of internal policy or institutional changes within Russia itself.

---

[1] Differences between the figures reported by the IMF and the Economist Intelligence Unit (EIU), on the one hand, and those of Goskomstat, on the other, are negligible.

The external circumstances contributing to growth most notably include the sharp rise in world market prices for oil and natural gas and their consequent effects on Russian export earnings. Another such circumstance affecting the Russian economy's favorable performance relative to that of the other G8 economies is the generally laggard growth of the latter.

Internal changes have included the ruble depreciation and monetary stabilization in 1998, simplification and flattening of the tax structure, and progress in marketization, privatization, and other reform measures that have stimulated entrepreneurship, start-up companies, and competitive markets.

The aim of this chapter is to determine how much of Russia's improved macroeconomic performance is plausibly attributable to the favorable (from Russia's point of view) external developments in global oil and natural gas prices. Toward this end, we computed several regression models in which we use annual and (separately) quarterly data to regress Russia's aggregate GDP growth on oil and natural gas prices, production, and exports. The results help to answer the question of how much of the variation in Russia's growth can be *explained* by changes in the independent variables (i.e., oil and natural gas prices, production, and exports). In this instance, just as in other regression analyses, "explanation" does not imply causation. Our regression results thus indicate the extent to which variations in the independent variables are associated with—although not necessarily caused by—variations in the dependent variables.

Table 3.1 summarizes the scale and importance of oil and natural gas in the Russian economy. As the table indicates, Russia's earnings from oil and natural gas exports increased from 34 percent to 55 percent of total export revenue from 1999 to 2005, a period in which oil prices rose by over 150 percent and natural gas prices rose by 40 percent.

Figures 3.1, 3.2, and 3.3 illustrate the links between oil and natural gas prices, production, exports, and Russian GDP growth. Table 3.2 summarizes the linkage regression calculations.

Figure 3.1 suggests that the relationship between oil prices and growth was generally close, with notable variations, during the 1995–

Table 3.1
Oil and Natural Gas in the Russian Economy, 1995–2005

Fossil Fuel	1995	1996	1997	1998	1999	2000	2001	2002	2003	2004	2005[a]
Oil											
Production (billion bbls)	2.19	2.14	2.16	2.14	2.22	2.36	2.52	2.70	2.99	3.21	3.26
Production value as share of GDP (%)[b]	0.04	0.05	0.05	0.04	0.02	0.06	0.05	0.05	0.07	0.07	0.11
Oil export revenue (billion $)[c]	18.35	23.41	22.06	14.51	19.61	36.19	34.36	40.37	53.74	78.56	109
Oil export revenue as share of total export revenues (%)	0.16	0.18	0.17	0.14	0.19	0.24	0.25	0.27	0.29	0.32	0.40
Natural Gas											
Production (billion cu. ft.)	21,010	21,230	20,170	20,870	20,830	20,630	20,520	21,040	21,780	22,133	22,111
Production value as share of GDP (%)[b]	0.06	0.07	0.07	0.06	0.06	0.08	0.08	0.06	0.09	0.09	0.09

Table 3.1—Continued

Fossil Fuel	1995	1996	1997	1998	1999	2000	2001	2002	2003	2004	2005[a]
Gas export revenue (billion $)	12.12	14.68	16.41	13.43	11.35	16.64	17.77	15.90	19.98	21.85	23.91
Gas export revenue share of total export revenues (%)	0.15	0.16	0.19	0.18	0.15	0.16	0.17	0.15	0.15	0.12	0.15

SOURCES: EIA database, http://www.eia.doe.gov/, January 10, 2006; CBR, http://www.cbr.ru/eng/statistics/credit_statistics/, January 2006.

[a] EIA estimate as of June 2005.

[b] The figures shown for oil and natural gas production value are gross rather than net—that is, they include the values of inputs to the oil and gas sectors (such as transportation and distribution costs) rather than being confined to value added by the oil and gas sectors. Nevertheless, the figures shown here for value as a share of GDP are likely to be underestimated for both oil and natural gas. In a February 2004 Economic Memorandum, the World Bank asserts that the reported low share is the result of transfer pricing and that the actual numbers are almost double the reported ones (http://siteresources.worldbank.org/INTRUSSIANFEDERATION/Resources/). The Bank attempts to calculate updated values using data from other countries and Russian trade data. However, values for all years are not computed, and only the manufacturing sector is considered in the calculations.

[c] Oil exports include oil and oil products as reported by the CBR.

Figure 3.1
Global Oil Prices and Russian Economic Growth, 1995–2005

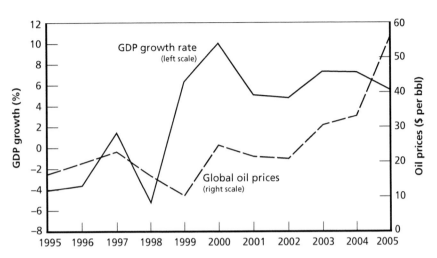

SOURCES: IMF, http://www.imf.org/external/country/index.htm, December 1, 2005;
EIA database, http://www.eia.doe.gov/, August 2, 2005.
RAND MG515-3.1

2005 period. Sometimes the two series track with one another, and sometimes oil prices lead growth or lag behind it. Figure 3.2 shows the intimate and sustained relationship between oil prices, Russian oil production, and Russian oil export revenue. As can be seen, supply curves are (usually) positively sloped: higher global oil prices generally lead to higher Russian oil production and higher export earnings.[1]

Russian production and exports of natural gas are another aspect of the Russian economy's dependence on fossil fuels. Figure 3.3 suggests the close link between global prices of oil and natural gas. Table 3.3 shows that the simple correlation between them is 0.773.

Table 3.3 is a correlation matrix showing the extent to which the components of the Russian fossil fuel sectors—prices and exports for both oil and natural gas—are tightly linked to one another. As can be seen, their respective simple correlations span a range between 0.78 and 0.79.

---

[1]   We assume here that other things are equal—e.g., that such exogenous factors as possible supply disruptions have not themselves contributed to the higher prices.

Figure 3.2
Global Oil Prices, Russian Oil Production, and Russian Export Revenues,
1995–2005

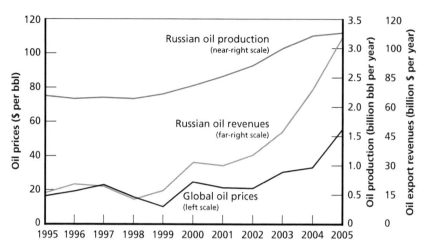

SOURCES: IMF, http://www.imf.org/external/country/index.htm, December 1, 2005;
CBR, http://www.cbr.ru/eng/statistics/credit_statistics/, August 10, 2005.
NOTE: Oil export revenues = oil exports × oil prices.
RAND MG515-3.2

Figure 3.3
Global Oil and Natural Gas Prices, 1995–2005

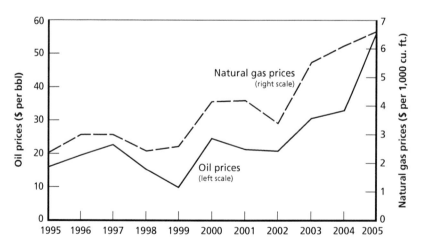

SOURCE: EIA database, http://www.eia.doe.gov/, August 2, 2005.
RAND MG515-3.3

Table 3.2
Russian Economic Growth and Effects of Oil and Natural Gas:
Regression Results, Annual Data, 1993–2005

Regression	Oil Prices	Oil Export Revenue	Gas Prices	Gas Export Revenue	R2	Adjusted R2	F-Statistic
			(Dependent variable is real GDP growth)				
I	0.710 (2.315)				0.328	0.267	5.360
II			2.440 (2.760)		0.409	0.355	7.617
III	0.241 (0.514)		1.868 (1.296)		0.424	0.309	3.686
IV		0.00007 (0.515)		0.001 (1.339)	0.528	0.433	5.591

SOURCES: (1) GDP growth data from IMF, http://www.imf.org/external/pubs/; (2) oil and natural gas export revenue data from CBR, http://www.cbr.ru/eng/ statistics/credit_ statistics/; (3) oil price data from EIA, http://www.eia.doe.gov/pub/ international/iealf/table71.xls; (4) natural gas price data from EIA, http://tonto.eia. doe.gov/ dnav/ng/hist/n9100us3a.htm.

NOTES: All variables measured in constant 2002 dollars. F-statistics significant at 5 percent level for all regressions except III, for which F-statistic is significant at 10 percent level. T-statistics (shown in parentheses) for regressions I, II, and III significant at 5 percent level.

The same regressions were run using quarterly data from 1994 Q1 to 2005 Q3 rather than annual data. The quarterly regressions lower the adjusted R^2 and hence the percentage of variance explained in the GDP series, because the quarterly data exhibit less variability than the annual data.[2] With less variability to be explained, the explanatory power of the regression is weakened when quarterly data are used.

To answer the question posed at the beginning of this chapter— To what extent has the Russian economy's strong growth resulted from oil and natural gas prices and revenues?—annual data are more appropriate than quarterly data. The reason why they are more appropriate

---

[2] The coefficient of variation in the annual GDP data is nearly four times as large as that in the quarterly data (7.1 versus 1.9). Regression results using quarterly data are shown in Appendix Table A.2.

Table 3.3
Oil and Natural Gas: Correlation Matrix, Annual
Data, 1993–2005

	Oil Export Revenue	Gas Export Revenue	Oil Prices	Gas Prices
Oil Export Revenue	1			
Gas Export Revenue	0.844	1		
Oil Prices	0.785	0.869	1	
Gas Prices	0.936	0.791	0.773	1

is that the ramified effects of oil and gas prices on other sectors of the economy—the forward and backward linkages between oil and natural gas and other sectors—and on investors' and consumers' expectations and behavior are more readily observable when sufficient time is allowed for the effects to be transmitted. These effects are therefore more discernible in annual rather than quarterly data.[3]

Several inferences can be drawn from Tables 3.1 and 3.2 and Figures 3.1, 3.2, and 3.3:

- Oil and natural gas prices explain between one-third and two-fifths of the variance in Russian economic growth over the 1993–2005 period, reflecting the range of the adjusted R^2 in the regressions of Table 3.2.
- Variations in oil and gas prices have the greatest explanatory power among the several regressions we tested.

---

[3]   This benefit is obtained at the sacrifice of a smaller number of observations in the annual *versus* quarterly data, requiring a larger adjustment in the corresponding R^2 for the regressions using annual data.

- Again, "explanation" for the variations in Russia's growth does not signify causation. Implicitly, the regression equations are reduced forms of more-complex causal chains in the Russian economy; a more complete model would show the connections between the oil and natural gas variables and employment and production in feeder industries, as well as their linkages to multilateral trade, foreign investment, and other macroeconomic variables.
- Nevertheless, the Russian economy's growth rate and trajectory clearly reflect its heavy dependence in recent years on fossil fuels. As indicated in Table 3.1, oil and gas production accounted for between 16 and 20 percent of Russia's GDP and between 44 and 55 percent of Russia's total export revenues in, respectively, 2004 and 2005. The build-up of Russian foreign exchange reserves from $25 billion in 2000, two years after the 1998 depreciation of the ruble, to over $225 billion in the second quarter of 2006 is a further illustration of this dependence.

CHAPTER FOUR

Markets and Reform

As discussed in Chapter Three, fossil fuel prices are important elements in explaining Russia's recent impressive economic performance. One question that remains is, How much of Russia's economic performance can be plausibly attributed to other factors—specifically to the economy's transition from centralized planning to decentralized decision-making; from resource allocation by the state and its bureaucracies to allocation through market-driven, business competition; and from state enterprise to private enterprise?

In the past decade, Russia has enacted numerous conspicuous economic reforms, including the sharp ruble depreciation in 1998 (referred to earlier, in Chapter Two) and the flat individual income tax of 13 percent and flat corporate tax rate of 24 percent that followed. Whether these reforms have, in fact, been fully implemented is less clear. For example, in some instances, local tax exactions may exceed the stipulated flat tax rate; in other instances, side payments may be demanded by tax collectors to "qualify" the taxpayer for the lower rate. It is also unclear whether and, if so, to what extent the incentive-enhancing effects of these publicized tax reforms have been offset by the detrimental effects of contemporaneous state interventions in the functioning of markets and businesses, such as business-permit requirements, company registration, and other bureaucratic obstacles to market entry and competition.[1]

---

[1]   Other examples are the government seizure of Yukos, Gazprom's expanded role in the oil and gas sector through its acquisition of oil producer Sibneft, and Putin's affirmation that the state should have predominant control over such "strategic" industries as aviation and

Some knowledgeable observers have asserted that the economic reform "that has actually occurred is far less than meets the eye" and that in reality "the Russian economy has not transitioned to democratic free enterprise, [while] structural militarization is alive and stirring" (Rosefielde, 2004, p. 134). These observers lament the failure of Russian economic reform to generate a clear and expanding "unified economic space" in which competition can thrive and prospects for sustained economic growth would improve. The severely critical observers include Andrei Illarionov, who resigned as Putin's personal economic adviser in protest in December 2005, asserting at the time that "not only economic freedom has disappeared . . . but political freedom is also gone."[2]

However, there are also knowledgeable observers who cite the progress achieved thus far and the prospects for further reform in the future, and who opine that "full fledged liberal arrangements can be expected ultimately to prevail in Russia. Russians send that signal in their many opinion polls."[3]

Some scholars who were once optimistic about Russia's prospects for continued economic reform and marketization have altered their assessments. This side of the debate's initial assessment was positive: the economic model adopted by Russia and other states in the Commonwealth of Independent States was moving forward to a growth-oriented model "with low taxes, social transfers and public expenditures," similar to the economic model adopted in East Asia. Since 2004, some have sharply reversed their opinions, adopting instead considerably more pessimistic views of Russia's economic, as well as political, outlook.[4] As

---

telecommunications. See "As Gazprom Grows, So Does Russia's Sway," *Los Angeles Times*, October 16, 2005.

[2]   Andrei Illarionov, "Russia, Inc.," *New York Times*, February 4, 2006.

[3]   Padma Desai, "Give Putin a Break," *Wall Street Journal*, February 2005.

[4]   Aslund's most recent assessment (2005), which is based on the perverse effects of Putin's political authoritarianism and aggressive attacks on the "oligarchs," privatization, and foreign investment, is distinctly pessimistic. This is in contrast to the positive view he expressed in a paper in 2003 (Aslund, 2003) and to the less-positive assessment of reforms he made in Putin's first term (Aslund, 2004).

these conflicting views suggest, the Russian economic scene is complex, the evidence is mixed, and the prognosis is unclear.[5] However, three key indicators suggest a significant degree of effective economic reform as a component of and contributor to Russia's macroeconomic performance in recent years and provide a modest basis for optimism about Russia's economic prospects: the rising number and proportion of Russian enterprises that are privately owned, as distinct from state owned and mixed public-private ownership; the similarly rising level and proportion of employment generated by private enterprises; and the recent boosting of Russia's sovereign debt status to investment grade standing by the securities' rating agencies (BBB by Fitch, Baa2 by Moody's, and BBB– by S&P).[6] These rating enhancements are significant in that they not only lower the cost to Russia of access to global capital markets, but also represent an objective, although modest, expression of confidence in the Russian economy's prospects.

Russia's official data on ownership and employment over the 1996–2005 decade are summarized in Table 4.1. Despite uncertainties about these data, the pattern of monotonic increases in the number of privately owned enterprises and of the level and proportion of total employment generated by them is noteworthy. It suggests an encouraging movement (although without assuring this movement's irreversibility) toward decentralized resource allocation and decisionmaking in the Russian economy—an indicator with political and social as well as economic significance for Russia's future development.

---

[5] One prominent adverse indicator has been the rapid *re*-nationalization of Russia's previously privatized large companies, including Gazprom, Rosneft, Vnesktorgbank, Sibneft, and Avtovaz. To some observers, this move is a harbinger of increased corruption in the future (see Illarionov's "Russia, Inc.," *New York Times*, February 4, 2006).

[6] Fitch Ratings, http://www.fitchratings.com/, 2005; Moody's Investor Service, http://www.moodys.com/cust/default.asp, 2005; Standard & Poor's, http://www.funds-sp.com/home.cfm, November 14, 2005. Fitch investment grade ratings of BBB– and higher indicate relatively low to moderate credit risk. Credit ratings express risk in relative rank order, which is to say they are ordinal measures of credit risk and are not predictive of a specific frequency of default or loss. Moody's investment grade rating of Baa2 signifies moderate credit risk; it is considered medium grade and, as such, signifies that investments may "possess certain speculative characteristics." An S&P rating of BBB– and higher signifies an investment grade of medium risk.

Table 4.1
Russian Ownership and Employment

Ownership Type[a]	1996	1997	1998	1999	2000	2001	2002	2003	2004	2005[b]
	Number of enterprises, in 1,000s (% of total in parentheses)									
State	322 (14.3)	233 (9.3)	143 (5.4)	148 (5.1)	150 (4.8)	151 (4.5)	155 (4.3)	157 (4.1)	161 (3.9)	159 (3.6)
Private	1,426 (63.4)	1,731 (69.1)	2,014 (73.9)	2,147 (74)	2,312 (74.4)	2,510 (75)	2,726 (75.8)	2,957 (76.9)	3,238 (78)	3,499 (79.2)
Mixed public-private	209 (9.3)	227 (9)	235 (8.6)	240 (8.3)	234 (7.5)	247 (7.3)	245 (6.8)	248 (6.4)	253 (6.1)	258 (5.8)
Other	293 (13)	314 (12.6)	338 (12.1)	366 (12.6)	411 (13.3)	440 (13.2)	468 (13.1)	483 (12.6)	498 (12)	501 (11.4)

Table 4.1—Continued

Ownership Type[a]	1996	1997	1998	1999	2000	2001	2002	2003	2004	2005[b]
	Employment, in 1,000s of persons (% of total in parentheses)									
State	27,720 (42)	25,904 (39.3)	24,295 (36.8)	24,437 (37)	24,365 (36.9)	24,223 (36.7)	24,192 (36.7)	24,015 (36.4)	23,724 (35.9)	23,500 (35.6)
Private	23,496 (35.6)	25,775 (39.1)	27,595 (41.8)	28,322 (42.9)	29,659 (44.9)	30,812 (46.7)	32,495 (49.2)	33,814 (51.2)	33,424 (50.6)	33,211 (50.3)
Mixed public-private	13,860 (21)	11,821 (17.9)	10,473 (15.9)	9,551 (14.5)	8,049 (12.2)	7,463 (11.3)	6,148 (9.3)	6,009 (9.1)	5,865 (8.9)	5,780 (8.8)
Other	920 (1.4)	1,098 (1.7)	1,449 (2.2)	1,653 (2.5)	2,254 (3.4)	2,212 (3.4)	2,524 (3.8)	2,513 (3.8)	2,887 (4.4)	2,901 (4.4)

SOURCE: Goskomstat, Russia in Figures: Moscow, 2002, for 1996–2002 data, and 2005, for 2002–2005 data.
[a] Goskomstat defines *state* property in the Russian Federation as assets owned by the Federation (federal property) as well as assets owned by subjects of the Federation—republics, territories (*kray*), regions (*oblast*), and autonomous regions (*okrug*). *Private* property is defined as asset ownership by citizens and legal entities, excluding property that may not belong to citizens or legal entities according to the law. Citizens and legal entities are the owners of property granted to them as contributions by their founders and of property acquired through other means. *Mixed public-private* property refers to property whose ownership is a combination of these two categories. The *other* ownership type comprises NGOs and foeign-owned enterprises.
[b] Goskomstat estimate.

As the table shows, the number of privately owned enterprises more than doubled between 1996 and 2005, rising to nearly 80 percent of all enterprises; whereas state-owned enterprises during this period shrank from 14 percent to less than 4 percent of all enterprises. The volume of employment in private enterprises grew by 41 percent; employment in state enterprises declined by 15 percent. The expansion of private enterprise that occurred—especially medium-size and small-scale enterprises—covers a wide range of both high- and lower-technology goods and services, including, for example, computer and information technology, financial services, engineering and construction, spare parts manufacturing, and repair and maintenance services.

Moreover, the data in Table 4.1 probably understate the actual growth of the private sector. Privately owned enterprises—particularly smaller ones, with 50 or fewer employees—are more likely to avert inclusion in the official data, choosing instead to pay a "protection" price to avoid taxes and to escape from myriad regulatory constraints that might be imposed on them if they registered in the official data.[7]

The data do not provide a precise answer to the question posed at the beginning of this chapter. However, they do suggest that one cardinal indicator of the progress of market-oriented reform—namely, the burgeoning of private enterprise—appears to have registered significant gains in the Russian economy in the past decade.

---

[7] This statement is based on private conversations between the principal author and economists at Russia's Institute of World Economy, Moscow, October 2005.

CHAPTER FIVE

International Transactions

U.S. policymakers are particularly interested in Russia's economic transactions with three differently situated countries or group of countries: the Central Asian states, Kazakhstan, Uzbekistan, Turkmenistan, Tajikistan, and Kyrgyzstan; the "proliferation-risk" countries, Iran and North Korea; and China. U.S. policy concerns relating to the Central Asian group stem from the possibility that economic transactions between Russia and these states may reflect aggressive Russian efforts to revive and expand Moscow's formerly dominant influence in Central Asia and to undermine U.S. efforts to enlarge its presence and influence in the region. Whether and when the implicit "zero-sum" premise underlying this concern (i.e., that expanded Russian trade implies diminished U.S. influence) is valid is not a question we are able to pursue in this chapter. A related and significant question, which we touch on below, is Russia's possible exercise of economic "leverage" on the Central Asian states, through manipulation of trade and investment transactions, whether or not such exercise would diminish U.S. influence. Indeed, this issue applies as well to Russian transactions with Ukraine and other European trading partners, where the volume of transactions is greater—especially to Russia's energy exports to these countries; this pregnant issue is not one we were able to address in this study.

The "proliferation-risk" label makes it evident why the United States has policy concerns relating to these countries. Economic gains realized by Iran and North Korea through trade, investment flows, and other transactions with Russia may directly or indirectly contribute resources for these two countries' nuclear or other unconventional weapons programs and for potential exports or leakage from these programs to global, stateless terrorist groups.

Finally, the particular interest in economic transactions between Russia and China reflects this dimension of China's "peaceful rise" to a position of increasing prominence in the global economy (see Zheng, 2005).

Table 5.1 summarizes available data on trade and investment flows between Russia and the Central Asian states, Iran and North Korea, and China.

Oil, natural gas, and other fuels make up the bulk of Russia's global exports. In 2000, these energy exports accounted for 50 percent of Russia's exports; in 2004, 55 percent. The next three largest export categories in 2000 and 2004, respectively, were metals (21 percent and 16 percent), machinery and equipment (9 percent and 7 percent), and chemicals (7 percent and 6 percent). Together, these categories accounted for 83 percent of Russia's total exports in 2004 to the countries shown in Table 5.1.

The majority of Russia's global imports fall into four categories: machinery and equipment, food and agricultural products, chemicals, and metals. In 2000, machinery and equipment accounted for 22 percent of Russia's imports; in 2004, 38 percent. Food and agricultural products accounted for 15 percent in 2000, 17 percent in 2004; chemicals, 12 percent in 2000, 15 percent in 2004; and metals, 6 percent in 2000 and 7 percent in 2004. Together, these four categories accounted for 77 percent of Russia's imports in 2004 from the countries covered in Table 5.1.[1]

Figures 5.1 and 5.2, along with Table 5.1, indicate that Russia's trade balances with the Central Asian states, the proliferation-risk countries, and China have, with few exceptions, been predominantly positive throughout the 1995–2004 decade. It follows that the eight countries are either debtors of Russia or have liquidated their debts to Russia by unrecorded resource transfers (e.g., hard currency transfers), or that Russia retains contingent claims on them. The data on invest-

---

[1]   Data on composition of trade were obtained from EIU's "Country Profile Russia" for 2005 (Economist Intelligence Unit, 2005).

Table 5.1
Russian Economic Transactions with Selected Countries

Economic Transactions with:	Amounts (current $, millions)									
	1995	1996	1997	1998	1999	2000	2001	2002	2003	2004
Kazakhstan										
Exports to	2,555	2,551	2,472	1,911	1,224	2,247	2,778	2,403	3,279	4,645
Imports from	2,675	3,054	2,746	1,914	1,402	2,200	2,018	1,946	2,475	3,479
Investment flows to	0.4	0.5	0.2	1.7	1.2	3.5	19.2	6.1	27.1	84.1
Kyrgyzstan										
Exports to	105	134.3	98.9	83.8	70.7	103	83.3	104	161	266
Imports from	101	174.5	190.8	204.1	109.3	88.6	61.9	74.2	104	150
Investment flows to	–	–	–	–	0.0	0.0	0.3	1	0.6	0.6
Tajikistan										
Exports to	190	218.0	229	221.4	222.3	55.9	69.4	67.9	128	183
Imports from	167	668.1	750.3	711	663.0	237	130	66	69.9	75.9
Investment flows to	–	–	–	–	–	–	–	0.1	0.0	3.1

Table 5.1—continued

Economic Transactions with:	Amounts (current $, millions)									
	1995	1996	1997	1998	1999	2000	2001	2002	2003	2004
Turkmenistan										
Exports to	93.1	154.6	164.0	131.8	167.3	130	140	143	222	242
Imports from	179	33.6	56.7	29.0	43.5	473	39.1	32.1	28.4	43.2
Investment flows to	–	–	–	–	0	2.943	1.280	0.855	0.857	1.865
Uzbekistan										
Exports to	824	1,191.3	962.2	533.2	264.1	274	409	453	512	767
Imports from	889	592.7	923.3	473.7	423.2	663	584	344	484	612
Investment flows to	–	–	–	–	0.3	0.9	0.4	2.027	0.582	138.547
China										
Exports to	3,371	5,155.9	4,084.3	3,169	3,527	5,248	5,596	6,837	8,252	11,691
Imports from	865	1,693	2,035	1,160	894	949	1,646	2,401	3,295	4,748
Investment flows to	22.9	–	–	–	19.54	16.23	29.76	38.65	54.3	–

Table 5.1—continued

Economic Transactions with:	Amounts (current $, millions)									
	1995	1996	1997	1998	1999	2000	2001	2002	2003	2004
Iran										
Exports to	249.0	644.0	704	517	417	633	904	757	1312	10,103
Imports from	27.0	49.0	25.0	28.1	69.6	53.6	34.5	50.9	62.8	102
Investment flows to	–	–	–	–	–	–	–	–	–	–
North Korea										
Exports to	70.1	577.2	81.0	56.5	49.1	38.4	61.8	68.7	111	205.0
Imports from	15.3	315.65	15.23	8.5	7.2	7.7	16.7	11	2.9	4.8
Investment flows to	–	–	–	–	–	–	–	–	–	–

SOURCES: Goskomstat, Russia in Figures 2002–2005, Moscow; ADB database, http://www.adb.org/Documents/Books/Key_Indicators/2005/default.asp, August 1, 2005; China Statistical Yearbook 1996–2004, http://www.stats.gov.cn/english/statisticaldata/yearlydata/, September 1, 2005; IMF, Direction of Trade Statistics 2003, Washington, D.C.

NOTE: Nominal exchange rates used for each year represent the average local currency/dollar ratio for the year and were obtained from the IMF World Economic Outlook database, http://www.imf.org/external/pubs/ft/weo/2005/02/data/index.htm, September 10, 2005.

Figure 5.1
Russian Economic Transactions (Imports and Exports) with Selected Central Asian States

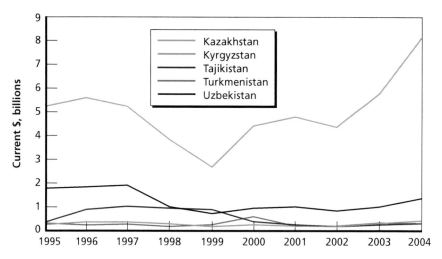

SOURCES: Goskomstat, Russia in Figures 2002–2005, Moscow; ADB database, http://
www.adb.org/Documents/Books/Key_Indicators/2005/default.asp, August 1, 2005.
RAND MG515-5.1

ment flows in Table 5.1 (from Russia to all but Iran and North Korea) indicate that Russia's acquisition of assets from these trading partners is small relative to Russia's trade balances with them. Assuming that the contingent claims Russia has accumulated in its trade with these countries are accurately portrayed by the table's data, one may conjecture that Russia has acquired some degree of economic leverage in its dealings with them. However, it should be acknowledged that this conjecture—that debtor status confers economic leverage on the creditor—is debatable; the other side of the debate may contend that the debtor can wield leverage through the threat of default.

A more benign interpretation of these data is also possible. To be sure, economic transactions have grown between Russia and the Central Asian states and between Russia and China. However, these trends may simply reflect Russia's economic growth and that of its trading partners, rather than portending some form of Russian economic "penetration." This benign interpretation is less plausible in the case of Iran and emphatically least plausible in the case of North Korea.

Figure 5.2
Russian Economic Transactions (Imports and Exports) with Iran, North Korea, and China

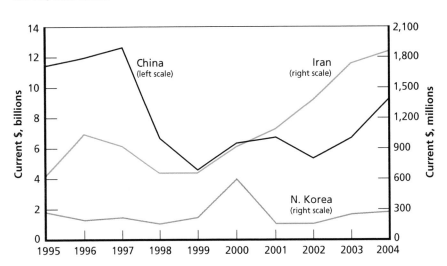

SOURCES: Goskomstat, Russia in Figures 2002–2005, Moscow; ADB database, http:// www.adb.org/Documents/Books/Key_Indicators/2005/default.asp, August 2005; China Statistical Yearbook 1996–2004, http://www.stats.gov.cn/englis, September 2005.
RAND *MG515-5.2*

Russia's evident use of gas as a "weapon" to influence Ukraine's resistance to Russian foreign policy in the early months of 2006 suggests that ascribing such benign intentions to Russia is unwarranted. Still, the strength of this particular weapon may be limited for cases in which fossil fuels are exported at world market prices, rather than subsidized ones, as prevailed in the Ukrainian case. Apart from the possible disruptions that can be brought about by using oil as a "weapon," an exporter's withholding of oil that is imported at market prices may, in the mid-to-longer term, simply lead importers to find replacement suppliers. However, Putin's assertion that "energy egotism is a road to nowhere" is as likely to be duplicitous as it is to be a reliable predictor of Russia's energy policies.[2]

---

2 Vladimir Putin, "Energy Egotism Is a Road to Nowhere," *Wall Street Journal*, February 28, 2006. This subject warrants much greater attention than we are able to devote to it in this monograph.

Turning to another dimension of Russia's economic transactions, arms sales, we summarize the data on the countries of interest (excluding Tajikistan and Turkmenistan, for which data were not available) in Table 5.2 and Figure 5.3.

Clearly, mixed motives underlie the growth of Russian arms exports to the countries covered in Table 5.2. The first and probably principal motive is to sustain and perhaps modernize the Russian defense industry. The prominence of this motive arises from the fact that domestic Russian demand for defense industrial output has been sharply reduced in both scale and priority from what it was before the Soviet Union's demise (see Chapter Six). A second motive is the role that arms sales take on as an instrument of foreign policy and as a reflection of Russia's continued aspiration to be a prominent player in the global policy arena. Profitability surely provides a third motivation, with manufacturers, government officials, and foreign firms often collaborating or colluding to fund arms sales wherever they can.

It is also important to note that in a period when U.S. arms exports have been rising (see Figure 5.4), it may be difficult to make a convincing case that Russia should not aspire to regain some of its prior (second- or third-level) ranking in global arms sales. To be sure, this does not gainsay that repercussions from Russia's arms sales may be worrisome and destabilizing from the U.S. viewpoint.

Table 5.2
Russian Arms Sales to Selected Countries

Country	Arms Sales (current $, billions)									
	1995	1996	1997	1998	1999	2000	2001	2002	2003	2004
Kazakhstan	0.1118	0.1955	0.1906	–	0.0744	0.1802	0.0389	0.106	0.0808	0.0361
Kyrgyzstan	–	–	–	–	–	–	–	–	0.012	–
Uzbekistan	–	–	–	–	–	–	0.0063	0.0064	–	–
Iran	0.0598	0.2692	0.2748	0.298	0.2927	0.3959	0.4418	0.4074	0.5511	0.349
N. Korea	0.0135	0.0161	0.0058	0.0059	0.006	0.0172	0.0301	0.0064	0.0065	0.0067
China	0.4245	1.2262	0.6373	0.1312	1.653	2.0762	3.661	3.038	2.5549	2.8896

SOURCE: SIPRI, Arms Transfers database, http://www.sipri.org/contents/armstrad/at_data.html#data, October 2005.
NOTE: Data on Tajikistan and Turkmenistan were not available as of the end of 2005.

Figure 5.3
Russian Arms Sales to Selected Countries

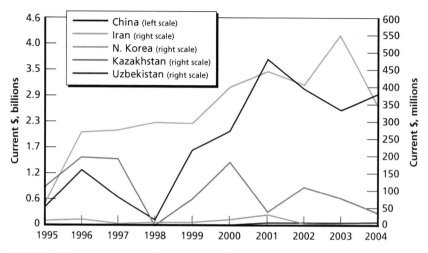

SOURCE: SIPRI, Arms Transfers database, http://www.sipri.org/contents/armstrad/at_
data.htm#data, October 2005.

RAND *MG515-5.3*

Figure 5.4
U.S. and Russian Global Arms Sales

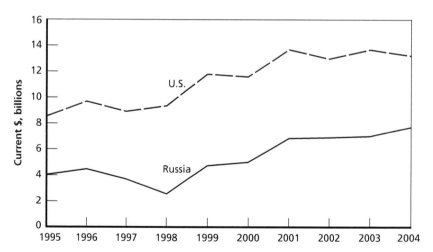

SOURCES: Defense Security Cooperation Organization Facts Book, http://www.dsca.osd.
mil/data_stats.htm, September 30, 2004; SIPRI, Arms Transfers database, http://www.
sipri.org/contents/armstrad/at_data.html#data, October 2005.

RAND *MG515-5.4*

CHAPTER SIX

Russian Military Spending

In the 1980s, during what was to be the Soviet Union's last decade, one of the principal controversies engaging the attention of analysts within the U.S. government and the academic community focused on measurement of the Soviet "defense burden": the ratio between Soviet military spending and the Soviet Union's GDP. Analysts especially skeptical about the validity of Soviet statistics contended that the defense burden was probably between 25 and 30 percent (Ericson, 1990; Epstein, 1990; Aslund, 1990). Other analysts, both within government and in the academic community, acknowledged that the Soviet defense burden was large relative to that of other countries but accorded more credibility to official Soviet statistics. They tended to make some adjustments to the statistics, emerging with defense burden estimates about half the size of the skeptics' estimate (Swain, 1990).[1]

Both the numerator and the denominator of the burden estimates were part of the controversy. The so-called "hard-liners" (including the principal author of this report) cited evidence indicating that the low-side estimates of military spending erred on two grounds: they did not sufficiently allow for the real value of top-quality inputs and products acquired in military spending (which would raise the numerator of the burden ratio), and they did not sufficiently account for the effects of hidden inflation, "value-subtracting" production, and resource misallocations on the real value of Soviet GDP (which would lower the denominator of the burden). The result of these flaws, they contended,

---

[1] See Rosefielde, 2004, chp. 3 ("Structural Militarization") for a comprehensive review and comparison of CIA and other estimates of the Soviet military burden.

was to underestimate the real military expenses and to inflate the estimated Soviet GDP—the denominator of the military burden—above its real value, thus lowering the estimated defense burden.

In any event, there is no doubt that the scale of military spending and the scale of the defense industrial sector in the current Russian economy have substantially declined from what they were in the Soviet era. Table 6.1 summarizes recent official data on Russian military spending and Russia's defense burden.

Any attempt to estimate Russian defense spending is complicated by the non-transparency of Russia's defense budget process. There are actually three defense budgets, each controlled by a different body: the federal budget that is voted by the Duma and becomes law; the real budget allocated to the Ministry of Defense by the Ministry of Finance; and actual spending by the Ministry of Defense. The budget is supposed to be implemented as enacted by the Duma, but it sometimes is not, because the government simply lacks the funds to fulfill its obligations. The Ministry of Finance disburses available funds, and the military then spends from these resources (Betz, 2000).

Russia's military spending is smaller and less opaque than was the case in the Soviet era, when defense spending data were secret. Nevertheless, Russia's official data remain considerably more opaque than do the corresponding data of most other major powers. As a consequence, the scale of Russia's actual military spending is assuredly larger than what the official data in Table 6.1 show.

For example, some outlays for military procurement and for military research and development are probably embedded in the budgets of federal departments and ministries other than the Defense Ministry. This was standard practice in the Soviet era and may continue, although to a lesser extent.[2] Still another inadequacy in the published data arises from the fact that Russia's armed forces are conscripted, which means that outlays for military manpower understate the true economic costs of the military. Were compensation to be based on the opportunity

---

[2]   See Rosefielde, 2004, pp. 96–98. According to one estimate, the Defense Ministry runs no more than 70 percent of actual defense spending, and the remainder is under the Ministry of Internal Affairs and the various KGB inheritors' budgets.

Table 6.1
Russian Military Spending and Defense Burden

	1995	1996	1997	1998	1999	2000	2001	2002	2003	2004	2005
Military spending, in:											
Current rubles	63.2	82.5	105	85.6	93.7	140.9	218.9	284.2	345.7	411.5	528
Constant 2005 rubles	559.3	506.3	562.9	394.6	261.8	282.7	372.8	423.0	451.5	455.5	528
Constant 2005 $											
Nom. exch. rates	15.0	17.2	19.0	9.1	3.9	5.0	7.3	8.7	10.6	13.2	16.9
PPP rates	213.0	133.2	130.2	76.3	64.0	58.3	72.9	57.0	73.2	69.5	61.7
Military burden, as %	4.1	3.8	4.2	3.1	5.0	4.0	4.1	4.4	4.6	4.1	2.9

SOURCES: IISS, The Military Balance 1995–2005, London, United Kingdom; Goskomstat, Russia in Figures 2002–2005, Moscow; GDP deflators and nominal exchange and PPP rates obtained from IMF World Economic Outlook database, http://www.imf.org/external/pubs/ft/weo/2005/02/data/index.htm, September 10, 2005.

NOTE: GDP deflators used for 1995, 1996, 1997, etc., through 2005 as reported by IMF; nominal exchange rates used for each year represent average ruble/dollar ratio for year; PPP between rubles and dollars for 1995, 1996, 1997, etc., through 2005 as reported by IMF.

costs of attracting equivalent manpower for a volunteer force, budgetary outlays would probably rise by, perhaps, 20 to 30 percent. Even without this imputed adjustment, the military burden figure for 2005 is likely to be at least as high as that for 2004—namely, 4.1 percent of GDP.

Table 6.2 shows Russia's defense spending compared with that of China, Japan, Germany, and the United States. Russia's current level of military spending is somewhere between $24 billion and $62 billion. Where it lies in this wide range depends on whether nominal exchange rates or purchasing power parity (PPP) conversion rates are used, whether considerations discussed above about military spending by non-defense ministries are taken into account, and whether proceeds from military exports are included (IISS, 2005). Russia's military burden is 4 percent of Russian GDP, representing either the fifth or second largest national total of military spending, after the United States and either ahead of or behind China and other countries, depending on different sources and ways of imputing dollar values to China's military outlays (Office of the Secretary of Defense, 2005; Crane et al., 2005).[3]

While Russia's "military-industrial complex" is undoubtedly sharply diminished in both role and scope compared with what it was in the Soviet Union, it remains a consequential factor in the Russian political-economic tableau. Rosefielde's assertion that Russia currently has "an intact military industrial complex" may exaggerate the reality (Rosefielde, 2004, p. 134), but Russia's defense industry is still the second or third largest supplier of arms in the global weapons market. Military exports from Russia to China of advanced weapon systems include jet fighters, guided missile destroyers, and more. Tables 6.3 and 6.4 summarize, respectively, Russia's global arms sales and the growth of these sales.

---

[3]   According to Crane et al., 2005, China's military spending in 2003 is estimated to have been between $31 billion and $38 billion. Official Chinese data place China's military spending in 2003 at $22.4 billion.

Table 6.2
Russia's Defense Spending Compared with That of Selected Countries

	Defense Spending (current $, billions)										
	1995	1996	1997	1998	1999	2000	2001	2002	2003	2004	2005
Russia	15.0	17.2	19.0	9.1	3.9	5.0	7.3	8.7	10.6	13.2	16.9
China	14.8	16.4	16.6	19	21.3	23.4	27.5	32.4	34.9	37.4	55.9
Japan	42.7	43.6	43.8	43.7	43.7	44	44.5	45	45.1	44.8	39.5
Germany	40	39.2	37.8	37.9	38.6	38	37.4	37.5	36.7	35.8	38.8
U.S.	355.3	336.1	334.4	326.6	327.6	340.2	342.9	385.1	437.4	480.6	402.6

SOURCES: SIPRI, Arms Transfers database, http://www.sipri.org/contents/armstrad/at_
data.html#data, October 2005; Office of the Secretary of Defense, Annual Report,
2004, http://www.defenselink.mil/execsec/adr2004/index.html; nominal exchange
rates obtained from IMF World Economic Outlook database, http://www.imf.org/
external/pubs/ft/weo/2005/02/data/index.htm, September 10, 2005.

Table 6.3
Russian Arms Exports

	Russian Arms Sales (constant 2005 $, billions)					
	1994–1998	1995–1999	1996–2000	1997–2001	1998–2002	1999–2003
China	2.91	4.60	6.59	8.96	11.30	15.45
India	3.77	4.77	4.52	5.19	5.39	8.56
Middle East	1.60	1.92	2.65	3.08	3.94	4.06
Latin America	0.69	0.84	0.86	0.91	0.61	0.54
Rest of world	7.89	7.98	6.95	5.73	7.28	11.55
Total world	16.86	20.12	21.58	23.86	28.52	40.15

SOURCE: SIPRI, Armaments, Disarmament, and National Security, Yearbooks
1998–2004.

Table 6.4
Russian Arms Exports, Average Five-Year Growth

	Average 5-yr Growth in Russian Arms Sales (%)	
	1995–1999	1999–2003
China	58	37
India	26	59
Middle East	20	3
Latin America	23	−12
Rest of world	1	59
Total world	19	41

SOURCE: SIPRI, Armaments, Disarmament, and National Security, Yearbooks 1998–2004.

CHAPTER SEVEN

Conclusions and Implications

Russia, with a GDP about one-fifth that of China but a per capita product twice that of China, is considered to have the second largest of the numerous economies considered to be "transitional." Exactly where it lies in the gamut of transitioning economies is not clear. Nor is it clear, though probably more important to discern, what the pace of the Russian economy's transition is and whether the transition is going forward, toward market-oriented, decentralized resource allocation; is going backward, toward centralized, state-controlled decisionmaking; or is, instead, oscillating between these two. These issues are deeply controversial and vigorously, sometimes vehemently, debated within Russia.

When each side of the debate looks at the data, it draws quite different inferences. The optimists contend that each step backward is more than offset by two steps forward, whereas the pessimists contend that each step forward is overbalanced by more than one step backward. For example, Russia's accumulation of over $225 billion of foreign exchange reserves from sharply increased fossil fuel prices and Russian oil and natural gas exports is viewed very differently by the two sides of the debate. One side sees the accumulation as a means of raising Russia's standing in international capital markets, thereby enhancing Russia's access to foreign capital, and as providing evidence that these resources will be husbanded for appropriate use as and when sound plans for social programs and infrastructure improvements are made. The other side sees the accumulation of these resources as evidence of a lack of sensible public policy and a failure to understand the compelling needs of the Russian economy and society. If these needs were duly recognized, this side contends, these idle resources could and should be employed to accelerate the pace of the transition.

In light of both the substance and the controversy described in our brief review of Russia's macroeconomy, the data and analysis in our study have led to the conclusions and implications summarized in the following paragraphs.

Russia's relatively impressive rates of real economic growth since 1998 have been substantially assisted by the escalation of oil and gas prices during this period. We estimate that between one-third and two-fifths of the variance in Russian growth is explained by changes in prices, production, and exports of fossil fuels. Thus, between 2 and 3 percent of Russia's average annual growth rate of 6.5 percent since 1999 is attributable to higher oil and natural gas prices and their associated export earnings.

Scenarios can be contrived that would sustain high real prices for fossil fuels—if not at the current $70/barrel price then, perhaps, in a range between $40 and $50 per barrel. However, the more likely scenarios—in our judgment—are those that will lead to lower prices. These downside scenarios could result from conservation and efficiency gains operating on the demand side of the energy market, in combination with expanded investment in oil and natural gas exploration and exploitation, along with increased refining capacity, as well as accelerated development of alternative energy technologies, operating on the supply side. We have not formulated these scenarios, but plausible circumstances along these lines could well lower oil prices to half of the current prices, or even further.

In consequence, if Russia is to sustain, let alone improve, its recent economic growth record, it must develop and implement economic and social reforms. Such reforms would accelerate the economy's movement toward more-efficient, competitive, and market-driven resource use in advance of a possible softening in the global energy market.

With this broad prospect in view, the evidence presented (see Chapter Four) of a seemingly strong and continuing growth of entrepreneurial activity is an encouraging signal for the Russian economy's future. Complementary policy measures would be invaluable in sustaining the further development of private enterprise—for example, fiscal policies to enforce the nominally simplified tax code, monetary policies to control the money supply and bank credit and to lower inflation, and regulatory and legal measures to enhance the stability and predictability of the economic environment. Such measures would encourage the continued growth of domestic Russian entrepreneurial activity, expansion of foreign direct investment in Russia, and joint ventures between foreign and domestic enterprises.

Russia's expanded economic relations with the Central Asian states and with China (see Chapter Five) should be viewed mainly as a reflection of the Russian economy's relatively high rate of economic growth, rather than as a significant instrument of economic "penetration" and enhanced Russian economic influence in these countries. However, in the case of Russia's economic relations with the two pro-liferation-risk countries, Iran and North Korea, expanded relations will inevitably add resources to these countries' ongoing and prospective weapons of mass destruction programs. This spillover effect is and should be of special concern to the United States. Whether and, if so, how the United States might induce Russia to expand its trade and capital flows to other countries and regions while reducing its transactions with Iran and North Korea are issues worthy of consideration, although they have not been considered in our study.

Finally, Russia's defense sectors—military spending, the defense industry, and arms exports—have plainly not prospered in the course of Russia's recent and continuing economic transition. Calling Russia's military-industrial complex "intact," as one observer did, may be an overstatement. But it is quite plausible that these sectors have emerged from the acute resource deprivation they suffered following the Soviet Union's collapse and are likely to realize at least modest and continuing benefits from the Russian economy's sustained growth. The ostensibly declining share of Russian GDP allocated to defense in recent years is likely to be reversed, resulting, instead, in at least modest increases in the coming years.

Appendix

This appendix presents three tables, the first of which, Table A.1, high-lights several facets of the calculations of Russian and Chinese GDP referred to in Chapter One.

Tables A.2 and A.3 supplement Chapter Three's discussion of relationships between oil and natural gas prices and revenues and the growth of the Russian economy. We found that regressions using annual data (see Chapter Three) rather than quarterly data (as shown

Table A.1
GDP Comparisons, Russia and China

	GDP (current $, billions)		GDP per Capita (current $)	
	2004	2005	2004	2005
Market exchange rate				
Russia	581.78	772.10	4,086.63	5,458.76
China	1,653.69	1,909.66	1,272.04	1,461.63
Ratio (Russia:China)	1:3	1:2.5	3:1	3:1
PPP rate				
Russia	1,449.17	1,585.48	10,179.44	11,209.40
China	7,334.25	8,091.85	5,641.63	6,193.42
Ratio (Russia:China)	1:5	1:5	2:1	2:1

SOURCE: IMF World Economic Outlook database, http://www.imf.org/external/pubs/ft/weo/2005/02/data/index.htm, March 2006.

Table A.2

Russia's Economic Growth and the Effects of Oil and Natural Gas: Regression Results, Quarterly Data, Q1-1993 Through Q3-2005

Regression	Oil Prices	Oil Export Revenue	Gas Prices	Gas Export Revenue	R^2	Adjusted R^2	F-Statistic
				(Dependent variable is real GDP growth)			
I	0.226 (2.094)				0.089	0.069	4.384
II			0.906 (1.650)		0.057	0.036	2.724
III	0.194 (1.759)		0.679 (1.229)		0.119	0.079	2.974
IV		0.0004 (2.301)			0.105	0.085	5.295

SOURCES: (1) GDP growth data from IMF, http://www.imf.org/external/pubs/ft/weo/2005/02/data/dbcoutm.cfm?SD=1995&ED=2005&R1=1&R2=1&CS=3&SS=2&OS=C&DD=0&OUT=1&C=922&S=NGDP_RPCH&CMP=0&x=55&y=7; (2) oil and gas export revenue data from CBR, http://www.cbr.ru/eng/statistics/credit_statistics/; (3) oil price data from EIA, http://www.eia.doe.gov/pub/international/iealf/table71.xls; (4) gas price data from EIA,http://tonto.eia.doe.gov/dnav/ng/hist/n9100us3a.htm.

NOTE: F-statistics significant at 5 percent level for regressions I and IV and at 10 percent level for regressions II and III. T-statistics (shown in parentheses) significant at 5 percent level for regression I and IV and at 10 percent level for regression II and oil prices in regression III.

here) explain more of the variance (as measured by adjusted R^2) in Russia's economic growth. To understand the difference between the results for annual and for quarterly data, we computed the coefficients of variation for all the variables. We found that in the case of the independent variables, there is little difference between the coefficients of variation for the annual versus quarterly data. However, we found that for the dependent variable (real GDP growth), the coefficient of variation is 3.5 times larger for annual than for quarterly data (7.059 compared with 1.945). Hence, there is more variance to be explained in the annual data, and the independent variables provide greater explanatory power in accounting for this variance.

Table A.3 is the correlation matrix for the regression covariates of Table A.2 using quarterly data for the period 1993 to 2005.

Table A.3
Oil and Natural Gas: Correlation Matrix,
Quarterly Data, Q1-1993 Through Q3-2005

	Oil Export Revenue	Gas Export Revenue	Oil Prices	Gas Prices
Oil Export Revenue	1			
Gas Export Revenue	0.755	1		
Oil Prices	0.948	0.772	1	
Gas Prices	0.200	0.122	0.234	1

References

Aslund, Anders, "How Small Is Soviet National Income?" in Henry S. Rowen and Charles Wolf, Jr. (eds.), *The Impoverished Superpower: Perestroika and the Soviet Military Burden*, San Francisco, CA: ICS Press, 1990.

———, "The Economic Resurgence of Russia, Ukraine and Kazakstan," paper presented at National Bank of Poland conference, October 2003.

———, "Russia's Economic Transformation Under Putin," *Eurasian Geography and Economics*, September 2004, pp. 397–420.

———, "Putin's Second Term Is Likely to Differ from His First: A Rebuttal," *Eurasian Geography and Economics*, 2005, pp. 435–438.

Betz, David, "No Place for a Civilian: Russian Defence Management from Yeltsin to Putin," paper presented at International Studies Association, 41st Annual Convention, Los Angeles, CA, March 14–18, 2000. Available at http://www.ciaonet.org/isa/bed01/.

Crane, Keith, Roger Cliff, Evan Medeiros, James Mulvenon, and William Overholt, *Modernizing China's Military: Opportunities and Constraints*, Santa Monica, CA: RAND Corporation, MG-260-1-AF, 2005.

Economist Intelligence Unit, "Country Profile Russia," 2005. Available at http://www.eiu.com (as of June 8, 2006).

Epstein, David, "The Economic Cost of Soviet Security and Empire," in Henry S. Rowen and Charles Wolf, Jr. (eds.), *The Impoverished Superpower: Perestroika and the Soviet Military Burden*, San Francisco, CA: ICS Press, 1990.

Ericson, Richard, "The Soviet Statistical Debate," in Henry S. Rowen and Charles Wolf, Jr. (eds.), *The Impoverished Superpower: Perestroika and the Soviet Military Burden*, San Francisco, CA: ICS Press, 1990.

Gaidar, Egor, "Recovery Growth and Some Peculiarities of the Contemporary Economic Situation in Russia," *Post-Communist Economies*, Vol. 15, No. 3, 2003.

International Institute for Strategic Studies (IISS), *Military Balance*, 2005.

Rosefielde, Steven, *Russia in the 21st Century: The Prodigal Superpower*, United Kingdom: Cambridge University Press, 2004.

Rowen, Henry S., and Charles Wolf, Jr. (eds.) *The Impoverished Superpower: Perestroika and the Soviet Military Burden*, San Francisco, CA: ICS Press, 1990.

Swain, D. Derek, "The Soviet Military Sector: How It Is Defined and Measured," in Henry S. Rowen and Charles Wolf, Jr. (eds.), *The Impoverished Superpower: Perestroika and the Soviet Military Burden*, San Francisco, CA: ICS Press, 1990.

Office of the Secretary of Defense, *The Military Power of the People's Republic of China 2005: A Report to Congress Pursuant to the National Defense Authorization Act*, Fiscal Year 2000, Annual Report, Washington, D.C.: U.S. Department of Defense, released July 19, 2005.

Yasin, Evgeny, "The State of Russian Economy in the Context of Past and Future Achievements," unpublished paper delivered in public lecture, 2005.

Yasin, Evgeny, and Andrey Yakovlev, *Competition and Modernization of Russian Economy*, Moscow, 2004.

Zheng, Bijian, "China's Peaceful Rise," *Foreign Affairs*, fall 2005.